Sam's Glasses

Written by Megan Basser
Illustrated by Teresa Culkin-Lawrence

It was the last day before school began, and Samantha was feeling grouchy. Tomorrow her class would have a new teacher, and Sam had a horrible feeling that it would be Mrs. Primly. "Please, please," she said to herself, "not Mrs. Primly! Everyone says she's strict and serious. She probably won't let us have any fun at all."

At school the next morning, Sam found her new classroom, peeped in, and groaned. There was Mrs. Primly, already writing notes on the board.

Then Sam saw that her best friend, Katy, was saving a seat for her. Soon they were chatting excitedly about their vacations, and Sam was beginning to feel much happier.

Sam almost forgot about Mrs. Primly until she heard a stern voice saying, "You two girls don't seem to be able to pay attention. Sam, please pick up your books and go and sit next to Philip Emery. You and Katy will have plenty of time to talk after school."

Sam picked up her books, hunched her shoulders, and slouched to the back of the classroom.

Sitting next to Philip was bad enough, but now Sam had another problem; she couldn't read the board from so far away. She asked Philip if she could see what he was writing, but Philip, who didn't like girls very much, covered his work so that Sam couldn't see it.

"Oh, please let me see," hissed Sam.

"No," smirked Philip. "Do your own work."

Finally Sam had to admit to Mrs. Primly that she couldn't see the board.

"Can you see, Philip?" asked Mrs. Primly.

"Perfectly," replied Philip smugly.

"May I suggest that you have your eyes tested, Sam? I'll write to your parents explaining that you can't see the board. For now, I think you should sit next to me," said Mrs. Primly.

Sam felt terrible. "I don't need glasses," she kept thinking. "Well, I hope I don't. They'll make me look stupid and ugly."

That afternoon, Sam told her parents about her first day back at school.

"It was awful!" she said. "My new teacher is Mrs. Primly and I just know that she doesn't like me at all. She's already written you a note saying that I need glasses. She made me sit at the back of the room. Then I couldn't read the board because she has tiny writing, and she doesn't press on the chalk hard enough."

"Well, Sam," laughed her father. "Mrs. Primly sounds very sensible to me. And we can soon find out whether or not you need glasses. We'll make an appointment with my optometrist and she can decide."

Sam didn't like going to school the next morning, but she came home feeling very excited. "We've been reading Cinderella, and Mrs. Primly thinks that our class should make the story into a play!" she said. "All the other classes and the parents will be invited to watch!"

"Perhaps Mrs. Primly isn't so bad after all," smiled her mother. "By the way, Sam, we've made your appointment with the optometrist for tomorrow after school."

"Oh no!" said Sam. "Can't it wait until after Friday? That's when Mrs. Primly's holding the auditions. If I have to wear glasses I'll never be chosen to play Cinderella. I'll probably have to be an ugly sister instead."

The next day Sam and her father went to the optometrist, who asked Sam to read a chart of letters on the wall. Sam could only read the first four lines.

Then the optometrist put a machine in front of Sam's eyes and asked her to read the chart again. She tried different lenses in the machine, and soon Sam could read the whole chart.

"Well, Sam," the optometrist said. "There's nothing seriously wrong with your eyes, but you are near-sighted. That means you have trouble seeing things that are very far away. If you'd like to choose some frames that you like, we can have your glasses ready in an hour."

Sam's heart sank.

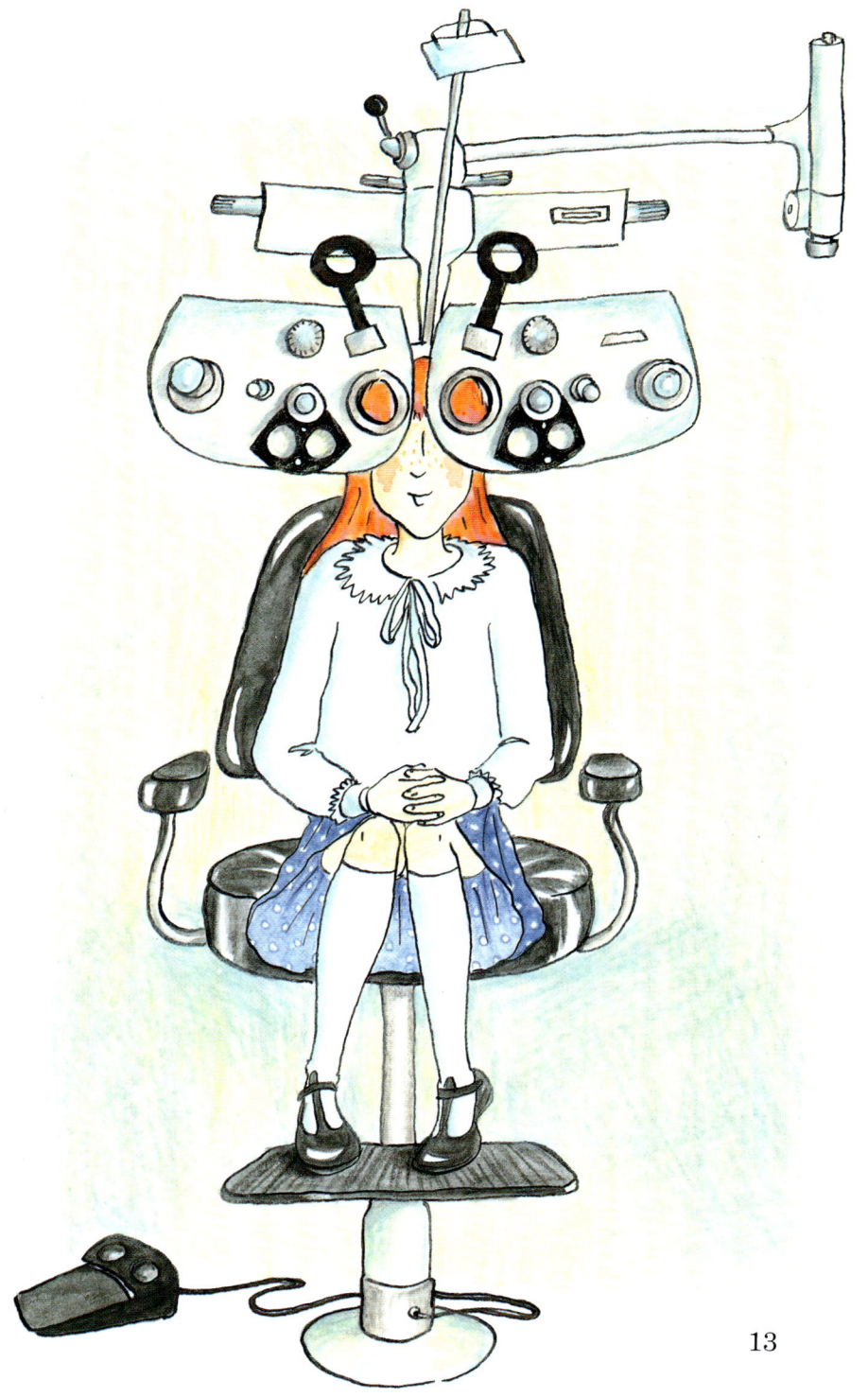

"Cheer up, Sam," said the optometrist. "You'll be amazed how quickly you get used to them."

Sam's father helped her choose a pair of bright blue frames. Then they read magazines together while they waited for Sam's lenses to be fitted.

After a while the optometrist called, "Your glasses are ready, Sam." Then she made sure that they fitted properly. They felt funny on Sam's ears and nose, but she had to admit that they didn't look too bad.

The next morning, Sam's mother had to call her five times before she'd get up.

"I don't feel very well. I think I should stay home today. I have a pain right here," she mumbled, pointing to her stomach.

"Well, come down to breakfast and then see how you feel," said her mother.

When Sam had eaten three pieces of toast and a bowl of cereal, her mother said, "Sam, are you really sick? I think that you don't want to go to school because you have to wear your new glasses."

"Do I have to wear them?" pleaded Sam. "All my friends are going to laugh at me."

"Yes, you do. Hurry up, and I'll drive you to school. You're running late," said her mother, smiling.

When Sam walked into the classroom, Philip Emery whistled at her.

Mrs. Primly said, "Philip, don't be so rude! Sam, your new glasses are very becoming. If you promise to be quiet you may sit near the back with Katy. Philip, you can sit next to me until you learn better manners."

Sam enjoyed the rest of her day. She made certain that Mrs. Primly didn't get angry with her for talking too much. And she could see the board easily.

At the end of the day, Sam rushed home to rehearse for the audition. She didn't think she'd be able to get the part of Cinderella, but perhaps Mrs. Primly would choose her as the fairy godmother.

Next morning Sam was very nervous. She'd carefully learned all her lines, but that wasn't the same as reciting them in front of the whole class — including Philip.

Sam was the last to audition. She tried to speak slowly and clearly. Then, when she'd finished, she sat down with the other children to wait for Mrs. Primly's decision.

One by one, Mrs. Primly read the names of the characters in the play and announced who would be playing each part. Sam breathed a sigh of relief as three other girls were given the parts of the ugly sisters, and she tried not to be too disappointed when Katy was named as the fairy godmother.

Soon there were only two more parts to be announced.

"I'm sure you'll all want to know who has been selected to play the parts of Prince Charming and Cinderella," said Mrs. Primly. "I have chosen Philip Emery to be Prince Charming — he read very well."

"Yuk!" thought Sam.

"And Sam, you'll be Cinderella."

"But . . . I . . . but you know that I can't see very well without my glasses. I'll have to wear them during the play."

"Of course, Sam," replied Mrs. Primly, laughing. "I can see no reason why Cinderella wouldn't wear glasses if she couldn't see very well."

Everybody agreed that the play was a huge success. Sam had learned her part perfectly — and she didn't even mind when Philip Emery kissed her on the hand.